This book is dedicated to Banksy and Popof. – FG

Phaidon Press Inc.
65 Bleecker Street
New York, NY 10012

Phaidon Press Limited
2 Cooperage Yard
London E15 2QR

Phaidon
55, rue Traversière
75012 Paris

phaidon.com

This edition © 2021 Phaidon Press Limited
First published as *Banksy* by Fausto Gilberti
Reprinted 2021, 2022, 2023
© Fausto Gilberti, © Maurizio Corraini s.r.l.
Published by arrangement with Maurizio Corraini s.r.l.

Text set in Raisonne Demibold and Fugue Regular
ISBN 978 1 83866 260 8
001-0423

Printed in China

Picture credit: Courtesy of Pest Control Office, Banksy,
London, 2004.

BANKSY

Graffitied Walls and Wasn't Sorry.

Fausto Gilberti

People know me as Banksy,
but that's not my real name.
That's just what I call myself.

Nobody knows who I really am,
and that way, I stay out of trouble.

Don't worry, I'm not a robber!

I'm an artist.
To me, nothing is as exciting as doing
a painting where nobody expects it!
I paint in the streets, on the walls of buildings,
the sides of houses, and underneath bridges.

My art is called graffiti.
I do it without permission
and I'm not sorry.

I make my art with spray paint and stencils.

I've painted monkeys, policemen, children,
soldiers, pandas, and the British royal family…
but I especially like painting rats.

Rats?

Yes, that's right—rats!

Rats run around cities,
they are everywhere and nowhere,
always causing a stir.
And, you know, that's a bit like me.

I once put 200 live rats in an art gallery.
Can you imagine what *that* was like?

I've painted all over the world.
I like to make images that say something,
that mean something.

They can be against war,
or poverty,
or pollution.
And a lot of the time,
about how I'm fed up with politics.

I've even done graffiti on a wall guarded
by soldiers armed with rifles. Luckily,
they were soldiers who liked my graffiti.

I don't just paint on walls.

One day I was in the countryside and I felt like painting, but there were no walls around me. So I painted on some cows and sheep.

Don't worry, though.
I used animal-friendly paint.

A lot of my graffiti gets painted over or destroyed. Some people even try and take it—along with the wall it's painted on!

So I decided to do paintings on canvas as well. But I hated the idea of selling my work to a snooty art collector, who would just have it hang over a fireplace.

I wanted to create artwork where everyone could enjoy it—like in a museum.
But most artists have to wait until they die to have their art exhibited in museums.

So I did it my way.

I put on a hat, a big coat, a fake nose, and a beard so that I wouldn't be recognized. Then I snuck into the British Museum in London … and put one of my paintings on a wall without permission.
No one noticed it for three whole days!

I did the same trick in other museums.
I've even added my own artwork
in the Louvre in Paris, and in the Metropolitan Museum of Art in New York!

Then I decided to have a proper exhibition at Bristol City Museum, in England.

This time, I got permission.

It was an incredible exhibition and a lot of fun...
Or so I'm told. I didn't stay to enjoy it, of course.

I showed sculptures like robot chicken nuggets, eating ketchup.
Dancing sausages.
Swimming fish sticks.
A leopard skin sleeping in a tree.
And a little rabbit filing its nails.

I hid my paintings among the old artworks in the museum.
You had to try and find the Banksys.

I like to see how the public react to my work.
So one day I put some sharks in a lake in
a park in London.

The ducks didn't seem to mind!

Once, in New York, I filled a truck with stuffed animals.
They were crying out to the people walking by,
because they were being driven off to be turned into
steaks and hamburgers.

It became the talk of the city.

FARM
FRESH
MEATS

I don't really like selling my work for lots of money.

When a very rich woman bought
one of my paintings for 1.4 million dollars,
an alarm went off and the canvas
self-destructed! It was destroyed by a shredder
I had installed in the picture frame.

I wish I could have seen her face.

One day, together with fifty-eight of my artist friends, I put together a non-amusement park in a seaside town in England.

With grumpy staff,
a terrifying merry-go-round,
a crumbling fairy-tale castle,
and some rather impossible
fairground attractions.

I called it...Dismaland. Get it?
Because it was so gloomy.

But people had fun anyway.

Dismaland

Like I said, my art is worth a lot but
I don't really like selling it for so much money.

So one day, I set up a street stall where
I sold my paintings for only 60 dollars.
Many people walked past the stall because
they thought the paintings were fakes.
Only eight pieces were bought that day.

When people found out that they had bought
real, genuine Banksy paintings,
they fainted with excitement!
And those who hadn't bought them?
They fainted from the shock of missing out!

You know, I've done a lot of things over the years, but I never thought I'd end up famous.

My work is known to millions of people and yet no one knows who I really am.
Not even my own parents!

But people like trying to find out.

So, who am I?

Some say I am a woman who,
even with a busy life,
finds time to graffiti.

Some say I am a musician who,
in between gigs and writing songs,
finds the time to be a street artist.

Some people say Banksy isn't just one person,
but a whole team of artists.

There are lots of different theories.
Some of them... pretty wild!

Here's something that *is* true:
I can't wait for someone to find out!
Because sometimes, beyond Banksy,
even I forget who I really am!

So, if you find out who Banksy is...
will you tell me?

MORE ABOUT BANKSY

Banksy is one of the world's most famous, and perhaps most controversial, contemporary artists alive today. His identity, however, is a closely guarded secret. No one knows for sure who the real Banksy is, though it is believed he was born in Bristol, England, around 1974.

Banksy's work first began appearing on walls in and around Bristol and in London during the 1990s. His art technique is a mix of spray paint and stencilling—a technique he picked up as a quick way to create art in a public space…and not get caught!

Banksy has gone on to paint on walls all over the world. His art is very recognizable for its dark comedy and important messages about the environment and politics. He is not only known for his famous murals but for his paintings, installations, and performance art.

People pay huge sums of money to own Banksy's work, but some think of it as vandalism. No matter what anyone thinks, by painting in public spaces and making art that is accessible to everyone, Banksy has changed the way artists' ideas can be shared. He continues to make his mark on walls around the world today, fueling conversations and debates, and inspiring people across the globe.

This mural (stencil painting on a wall) by Banksy is called *Girl with Balloon*. It originally appeared on Waterloo Bridge in London in 2004. Although it was later painted over by local authorities, it remains one of Banksy's most iconic images, and was voted as Britain's best-loved artwork in a 2017 poll.